CHICKENBONE LAKE

**Myths,
Fishing Stories,
and
Theological Asides**

by Jonathan Sams

To Cheri: Will the Circle Be Unbroken

and

With gratitude to the people of
St. Timothy's Episcopal Church,
Griffith, Indiana

Library of Congress No. 88-082642
ISBN No. 0-9621417-4-7

ABOUT THE AUTHOR

Jonathan Sams is the Rector of St. Timothy's Episcopal Church in Griffith, Indiana. He has also written *Reflections of a Fishing Parson* and articles in *Field and Stream* magazine and other periodicals.

He lives with his wife Cheri and their two children, Caitlin and James Henry, in Merrillville, Indiana.

ABOUT THE ILLUSTRATOR

William Sauts Netamux´we Bock has illustrated many books, including *The Bread Sister of Sinking Creek* and *Maggie Among the Senecas* by Robin Moore. He has written and illustrated the *Wik´-wum Life Series: Traditional Ways of Living and the New Earth*, and is part of the Lena´pe Cultural Council and Native Scholars Network.

He is a Lutheran minister and lives with his wife and two children in Souderton, Pennsylvania.

TABLE OF CONTENTS

I

CHICKENBONE LAKE

I

Old outdoor magazines, piled in corners of the summer cabin, musty with river-smell and many winters of neglect: these were my primers, my consolation on the rainy mornings when we could not fish or swim or play. I would read of blackfish off a rocky coast, of high meadow trout, or giant marlin in some southern sea. But the place to which my thoughts returned, of which I re-read again and again was Chickenbone Lake.

Chickenbone Lake, where the fish are always hungry, the water always clear, and the pines keep watch along the shore. A montage of pike shape, habitat, and demeanor endures still in my imagination, drawn from the vivid watercolor of a lunging pike on the first page of the article, with the anonymous anglers shown in the distance, rods aloft, mouths agape. Around them the surface of the water was broken with the twisted shapes of fallen timber. Against this backdrop a typical fishing tale was told: a remote lake, an elaborately planned expedition, the initial suspense of fishing unknown waters, and then the fabulous success. These themes intrigued me, as they do still, but what haunted my imagination were the fish, the Great Northern Pike, the Water Wolves, lean and lurking, in the deep secret waters.

I suspect that much of the spell which Chickenbone Lake cast over me came from the context in which I learned of it: the boyhood years in the summer cabin, the handpump in the frontyard, the cousin-filled summers, the inevitable night choirs of frogs and bugs, the creaking of the porch swing and the low voices of the adults as we fell asleep, and always, behind all else, the River, the Delaware, on its relentless journey to the sea.

Of course we fished all the time, every day, just about. We caught smallmouth bass, sunfish, chubs, rock bass, walleyes and even an occasional pike. All the productive holes and spots had special names, and the various expeditions over the years acquired legendary status, like "the time Cousin Topper caught the Pickerel," or "the time we got rained on at Muskrat Island." Given all that high-energy fishing experience, I wonder why I still went in thought so often to that brooding shore, those teeming waters? At times it seemed as if Chickenbone Lake were more real to me than our own Delaware River.

To this day, fishing good water, I will keep working my way downstream, wading or in my canoe, convinced in some corner of my brain that around the next bend waits a hidden, unfished pool, haunted with fallen timber, the perfect pike hole, my own "Chickenbone Lake." I become entirely caught up in this rhythm of quest and technique, trying each angle and each pike-fishing trick on every piece of likely-looking cover. Time becomes compressed, and it is always with reluctance that I disengage myself from that underwater world and return to this ordinary plane. New spots, new fishing possibilities, stir my imagination and entice me out early, while the mist rises heavily from the water and my ears strain against the morning stillness for the sound of predatory fish feeding in the shallows. I seek out rivers and bayous and small ponds, not vast, wind-swept lakes. I like to study the texture of the water, the cover and the bottom, and diagnose it as pike habitat. I like to hear and see the fish, even if I don't catch them. As I wade or float, cast and fool with lures, I think I go through a kind of merging with the fish, I almost *am* a fish, in some dim, dreamish section of my mind.

II

And, sometimes, I even *catch* fish. My wife's parents lived for a time near Calgary, Alberta, where we visited them. Behind their house was a steep drop-off and at the base, a shallow pond, the work of beavers, we supposed. I thought of it as potential trout water and so went forth, bearing a box of spinners and small lures. It was a bright, clear day, and as I stood below the beaver dam examining a shallow pool I beheld a familiar sight: a pike, about six inches long, which meant, of course, that grown-up ones might be around, and be caught, provided that a way could be found to approach the deeper water. Those who have fished beaver ponds will know that this can be difficult. I finally found a way to wade through the boggy ground below the dam (through several hip-deep holes of icy water) to a spot right up against that structure, which I could lean against and cast into an open space in the brush and standing trees where the water looked about four feet deep. I tied on a small rapala, which I thought would fish well in the snaggy water, and took a cast. No sooner had I begun the retrieve when a large pike emerged from the shadows to seize the lure and head back toward the heavy brush. My heart pounding, I leaned back on the rod to turn the fish, only to see the line part and the fish disappear into the depths. All this had taken only the briefest second. I stood still for about five minutes, calming myself and waiting for the pool to settle. Then I tied on my only other pike-sized lure, a diving rapala this time. I have often found that pike operate in packs, and I supposed that these Albertan fish might be the same. I cast again, and watched the lure dive as I cranked the reel handle. Well, another fish struck, and I set the hook hard. This time I played it delicately, steering it around the underwater obstacles and holding the rod high whenever it would catapult into the air or thrash on the surface. After about fifteen minutes (or so it seemed--who looks at their watch?) I was able to bring the exhausted fish up next to the dam, and since I had no net, used a stick from the beaver dam to heave it over into the shallow water on the other side. Holding the heavy fish up I saw a peculiar sight: two lures hung from its mouth, both of which, of course, belonged to me.

We ate that greedy fish, and rejoiced in it, and gained strength. But fish are not capable of greed, only instinct, hunger, and stealth: it takes a human being to transmute such energies into greed, as I did on one particularly fine evening on the Kankakee River in Indiana, where a friend and I had paddled far back in the bayous to fish for hidden pike. The very air seemed alive that time, the water and weather perfect for this quest. I lowered my large live minnow-bait into the water and at once had a strong young pike on the line. Upon landing it I could see that it was most likely not of legal size, but in my mind this was a night for a stringer-full, and so I was determined to measure this fish in case my eyes were deceiving me. As I reached into my tackle box to fetch the tape, the fish began to thrash around the bottom of the boat. Instinctively I jerked back, and came up with a large treble hook deep in the palm of my left hand. After some unpriestly words I set about trying to remove it, but not before I had measured the fish, found it wanting and thrown it back. While I was pulling and pushing at the imbedded hook, I let my line with a bare, unbaited hook dangle in the water beside the boat: another fish struck this, which I also brought in and released, all the while with a large lure dangling from my hand, bristling treble hooks. In the end we had to paddle out to where our car was, load the boat, and drive to the nearest hospital, where the sympathetic Chinese doctor looked at me quizzically and said: "How you do this?" I explained about legal size limits and sound conservation practice and he responded: "So, you are a purist." I did not disagree, but neither did I confess to him my haste, greed, and carelessness which had subverted our fishing on an evening when the fish didn't even require bait to strike. The doctor finished by saying, "Let me tell you something: when I catch 'em, I cook 'em."

I wish I could say I learned humility from that one experience. But only last summer I visited another emergency room with the same kind of lure hanging from my hand, caused by my overanxious handling of a twelve-inch pike. I was convinced there had to be a bigger one in the same cove, and my haste and greed betrayed me again. The doctor at that hospital had just read in a medical journal about a new technique for removing a fish hook, which consisted of looping suture thread around it and pulling real hard. I missed my non-purist Oriental.

III

These are not so different from all my visions and quests. I went into the ministry to proclaim good news to the poor and baptize the longing multitudes with living water; and I find myself mopping up drainwater in the parish hall so the new tile won't come up.

I became a parent to participate in the mystery of creation, to have a hand in the formation of new persons; and find myself indispensable usually when it's time to delve into the mystery of diaper changing.

I got married to pursue a deep need for intimate community; many times the living out of it means being intimate with a scrub brush as I take my turn cleaning the bathroom.

As for Chickenbone, I'll never try to go there, to the "real" Chickenbone Lake, I mean. I prefer to search for my version of it in the waters that surround me now. My Dad used to chuckle when I would persuade him to read the magazine story out loud because the author mentioned almost in passing that his first trip to the fabled lake, undertaken with a full complement of fishing companions and guides, was a failure. It seems they had forgotten all their fishing tackle.

My brother Bob says that "religion is what happens when myth and reality intersect." That is what I expect these stories to be about: enchanted lakes and forgotten fishing gear; shimmering, unfished beaver ponds and bumbling anglers who wear their tackle dangling from their bodies like sacred charms; about Jesus, the consummate fisherman and perennial physician, and the church, his reluctant bride; and God, always verging on the present yet always just beyond, where the fish are always hungry, the water always clear, and the pines keep watch along the shore.

II

THE GREAT DELAWARE RIVER
FLOAT TRIP

When most people use the word "myth," it is simply to denote something untrue, outdated, or unbelievable. Others have a different definition, such as W. Taylor Stevenson, who in an article in *Cross Currents* wrote in 1970:

> Briefly stated, myth performs two functions for the community which adheres to it: it reports the "true story" of events which "actually took place"; and it sets going concrete sacral forces which structure man's world intellectually, emotionally, and socially. Further, because myth is *the* true story, it is all embracing and cannot be explained in terms of stories or categories more fundamental than those of the myth.

When Bob Sams speaks of "myth intersecting with reality," I think what he means by "reality" is our modern view of scientific facts and verifiable events, where we analyze even our own analyses in a never-ending quest for what's valid and predictable. But perhaps (as Taylor Stevenson suggests in his book *History as Myth*) even our version of "reality" proceeds from our own equivalent of "myth." We have to start somewhere, after all, with what is believed to be the "true story" of reality, a "platform" from which to perceive and interpret the rest of our experience.

Can our fishing stories come to have this kind of power for us? To "structure" our world "intellectually, emotionally, and socially"? That may be asking a bit much of them, but perhaps they can, in their measure, as I shall try to tell.

A few years ago Bob and his son Ben, my sister Casey and her husband Andy, and I made a float trip on the Delaware which was to take us from the mouth of Broadheads Creek, down through the Delaware Water

Gap, and bring us out at our Aunt Shirley Wheeler's house at Slateford. As kids at the summer cabin we used to gaze downstream and wonder what lay around the bend, but the swift water and our small boat and motor precluded our going down to see. We actually came to have a kind of superstitious awe of those unknown waters, although there is really no great mystery about it, as thousands of canoers pass through there every year, and it is all part of a heavily-utilized National Recreation Area. But to us it was all new water, and we set out with high hopes on an utterly sunlit August day, the water sparkling and clear, reflecting with stark clarity the deep blue of the sky and the steep cliffs of the Jersey Shore. In a short time we had filled our stringer with the fattest of our catch of bluegills, rock bass, and perch. In the fast water we also were getting strikes from smallmouths, and I steered us stern first through the rolling current so Bob and Ben could aim casts behind the big rocks as we moved swiftly past. This was an exciting boat ride, as well as fishing trip, and we were all caught up in the power and varied beauty of the River. Casey and Andy followed behind us in a canoe, so we could observe each other's helmsmanship as well as fishing. At about mid-point, somewhat downstream from the Interstate Highway Bridge, a fresh set of rapids begins, and Bob took over at the oars and I replaced him in the bow. As we entered the fast water I cast my oversized rapala behind a large boulder, and at once an equally oversized smallmouth hit it and leapt high out of the water, presenting himself broadside for us all to behold, and our voices mingled in a shout that hung for a moment like the old bass, suspended between water and sky. This was, I knew, the biggest bass of my fishing life, and I fought him slowly, on a long line, while Bob guided us in between the foaming rocks and the fish returned again and again to the air in mighty leaps. In the end we had him, as the rapids slowed and we beached on the point of a small island. Nineteen inches long, probably over five pounds, a heavy, crayfish-gorged Granddaddy Bass, a Lord of Waters and Source of Tales.

All this we saw with our own eyes, but also, in a way, through Ben's, as our Dad must have viewed those expeditions from the past through ours. We floated on

through tamer water, ourselves subdued now as Slateford came into view below, and the Great Float Trip ended, and verged over into that place where our lives turn into stories.

What happens to us when we retell this story? Does it serve to "structure our world" and "report the true story"? Does the telling renew the bonds among us, among all who have floated or have fished? Does it evoke in us the memory of our ancient kinship with the fish, with whose evolutionary ancestors ours parted company to make their damp living in the primeval swamp? In the telling does our circle widen and permit us to join the Indians, the Lenape, as we ply their waters in our aluminum version of birch bark?

SMALLMOUTH BASS

It does for me. And the memory of it enters my dreams, and I am swept downstream through the ancient Gap toward a place where all the stories and the rivers merge, and sleep rolls like breakers on an unknown shore.

III

MYTH AND REALITY:
GREAT LAKES SALMON

In spring . . . when the salmon begin to run up the Klamath River, the Karoks of California dance for the salmon to ensure a good catch. One of the Indians, called the *Karega* or God-Man, retires to the mountains and fasts for ten days. On his return the people flee, while he goes to the river, takes the first salmon of the catch, eats some of it, and with the rest of it kindles the sacred fire in the sweating-house. No Indian may take a salmon before this dance is held, nor for ten days after it, even if his family is starving (Frazer, 1963).

That's one way to look at things. Another way is after the fashion of whatever astute employee of the Department of Natural Resources (in Michigan, I think) it was who kept hearing about all these dead minnows that were piling up on the beaches down by Chicago, and somehow got the idea of transporting migratory trout and salmon from the Pacific Northwest into the Great Lakes, which, if the transplant worked, would reduce the alewife population by natural predation and, incidentally, provide some sportfishing possibilities as well. What followed is one of the great triumphs in modern management of outdoor resources. The coho, chinook, steelhead, and brown trout transferred their anadromous habits to the Great Lakes and its tributaries without a hitch. They do not (except in a few streams in Michigan) reproduce naturally, so their numbers have to be continually re-stocked from artificial sources, but this added expense to the state is minuscule in comparison with the wealth of the recreation industry that has grown up around these fish. Thousands of people make their living from it.

I contribute to this industry each year with my purchases of licenses, lures, large landing nets and the other accoutrements of such fishing. Throughout the Fall I range the small Indiana creeks that enter Lake Michigan from the south, watching the water for the telltale bulges that indicate the presence of large migrating fish in the narrow stream. At times the fish jump clear of the water, and since some weigh forty pounds, they create no small splash. Sometimes several of these large fish will begin writhing and swirling around a certain pool, whipping the water to a froth in some mating ritual, I suppose. And the fish themselves are amazing to see. The salmon are silver, often massive, and acquire a dark blue or even blackish hue as the season wears on. Toward the end of the run, they even begin to decay and drag their cadaverous bodies over the snags and other water-obstacles driven by a relentless urge to continue on upstream. The steelhead are the most impressive to me, with various hues of pink and red gill plates and broad stripes. They strike a lure with savage power, almost tearing the rod from one's hands. I once hooked a steelhead at a bend in the creek, only to have it race back downstream around the bend and out of sight. All I could see was my arching rod and the line stretched taut downstream while the drag screamed on my reel and I hung on bewildered. The next thing I saw was the fish swimming back up past me, still hooked but with my line stretched out the opposite way, evidently wrapped around some tree limb beyond the bend. The fish then vaulted out of the water, shook its head, and threw the lure right at my ear. All this took only a few seconds.

I have caught other steelhead, and salmon too, in these narrow, sluggish Indiana creeks. But the chief pleasure I have gained from them has been to bring certain friends and show them these migratory fish in such unlikely surroundings. One such friend is Mark Johnston, a fellow cleric who has shown me many deer stands and fishing holes in his Alabama territory, and I had looked forward for a long time to returning the favor. It was cold October the day we fished, itself an oddity for a southerner like Mark, with the autumn foliage falling copiously into the water to foul our hooks. I kept seeing fish as they passed by, or their wakes, rather, and the tips of fins or wide backs as they rolled over logs. I tried to point them out to Mark, but he wasn't sure what I was looking at, and grew more skeptical as the day wore on. As he put it later, "it was *boring*," which, I believe, may be a moral preliminary to all genuine fishing or hunting success, because late in the afternoon, retrieving a cast no different from any other he had taken all that day, a steelhead struck, and I heard him shouting, "Jon, come quick! I've got a *huge* fish on here!" Since I had the net, I dropped everything else and began running headlong through the thick woods. When I came to the place where he was, the fish was still on, thrashing in the middle of a large pool. After several strong runs and horsing the steelhead away from some threatening snags, Mark brought it close enough so I could reach it with my long-handled net. Then I pitched the net and fish together over my shoulder onto the bank above. It weighed about eleven pounds. They get bigger, of course, but it was the largest fresh-water fish that Mark had ever caught. And Mark has caught a lot of fish.

So who's got the "true story" about the salmon? The Karok Indians or the Michigan DNR? Do Mark and I have anything at all in common with the *Karega*, as we go down to the creek with our elaborately designed fishing gear in pursuit of our scientifically managed fish? I hope so, in our fashion. I like to think that all of us midwestern steelhead and salmon fish folk are partaking in our own elaborately contrived salmon-dance, by the shores of the tributary creeks, on the charter boats, even at the cash registers of the sporting goods stores.   I think that perhaps we are all participating in what theologians have called a "second naïveté," a more or less self-aware return to that sacred version of the world, where the salmon are not merely pawns in an economic game but relatives sent to bless us. Perhaps we can be suffered to stand by the creek as the great fish slip by and murmur (under our breaths, so as not to be taken for lunatics) the old Indian Prayer of the Pacific Northwest: "You fish; You fish: you are all chiefs; you are; you are all chiefs" (Frazer, 1963).

COHO SALMON

IV

MORE SALMON MYTHS
AND REALITIES

In a canyon near the head of the river, there was a wonderful place that the tribespeople could always visit to find salmon . . . the villagers who lived nearby were wealthy enough to trade with others and much respected. As time went on, the younger people forgot the old traditions; sometimes they killed small animals and left the carcasses for the crows and eagles to eat. Their elders warned them that the chief in the sky would be angered by such foolish behavior, but nobody heeded them. In one case, when the salmon season was at its height and the fish were swimming up river in their myriads, some of the young men of the wolf clan thought it amusing to catch salmon, make slits in the fish's backs, put in pieces of burning pitch pine, and put them back in the water so that they swam about like living torches in the river . . . At the end of the salmon running season the tribe made ready for the winter ceremonies. But as they prepared they heard a strange noise in the distance, something like the beating of a medicine drum, and grew worried . . . The old people guessed that the young men's thoughtlessness in ill-treating the salmon had brought

trouble on the tribe . . . Eventually a noise like
thunder was heard, the mountains broke open, and
fire gushed forth until it seemed that all the rivers
were afire. The people tried to escape, but as the
fire came down the river, the forest caught fire and
only a few of them got away. The cause of the
conflagration was said by the shamans to be entirely
due to the anger of the spirit world at the torture of
the salmon . . . (Burland/Wood, 1985).

This is a potent story for our own times. Our
longsuffering environment, when abused, turns on us to
exact its retribution. Can we learn again to reverence
the earth and its inhabitants, and pass on the wisdom of
the elders to the young?

I will think of this story the next time I watch the
salmon making their laborious way up the narrow creek
to their inborn destiny. As much as I respect the fish,
and appreciate their presence and the human ingenuity

it took to put them there, in some ways it seems like a cruel joke to play on a wild creature. The huge energy they put into their upstream journey is all for naught. All the reproductive energies of nature are focused in that frantic determination. Little do they suspect that their great watery trek is a huge exercise in corporate sterility. The headwaters of these Indiana streams are too warm, too muddy, and too dirty for natural reproduction of these species. So their great sexual enterprise is doomed. "It's no use, guys," I mutter, as I observe their urgent striving.

I am not such a purist as to advocate that the salmon and steelhead programs be curtailed because they unfairly frustrate fish. But I do believe there are limits to how much we can regard the natural environment as a resource to be exploited with no restraint but our own good pleasure. At what point does our rearranging of the natural order cross the boundary into sacrilege? What is our equivalent to sticking torches in the salmon's backs? It is a perennial question for those who seek to keep faith with the earth as well as make use of it.

Lacking a definitive answer, I often seek consolation by going fishing, usually in the company of others who fish with integrity, with reverence for the fish and respect for the traditions of their fishing elders. One such companion of mine is Kevin, an agile youth who fishes while dangling from a tree over the creek, sort of like a human kingfisher. He keeps his legs

hooked around the trunk, which leaves his arms more or
less free to cast. From up there he can usually spot the
shadowy forms of the fish as they make their way up the
center of the stream, and for some reason they are less

aware of what's directly overhead than of activity along
the banks. In any event, he gets more strikes and hooks
more fish than anyone else. I say more strikes because
he has more difficulty landing the fish with his legs and

arms wrapped around this tree. Most often he'll start hollering for someone to come running with a net, and sometimes we hear him, sometimes we don't.

Kevin is a good fisherman, with good fishing instincts and attitudes. I think he has an unconscious affinity for the fish, a spiritual relationship that he takes for granted. Some people I've fished with have that gift; others have it for awhile and lose it; others never seem to have it at all. If Kevin were a twin I'd have an easy explanation, because "in the opinion of the Kwakiutl Indians of British Columbia twins are transformed salmon; hence they may not go near the water, lest they be changed back into the fish" (Frazer, 1963). I guess it's just as well he's not.

V

". . . I HAVE CALLED YOU FRIENDS"
(John 15:14)

I

Telling about Kevin perched in his tree like a latter-day Zacchaeus on the lookout for Christ makes me think of another time and another fish, of muskies, the godfathers of the pike family, and of the unseen bonds of tested friendship.

The first musky I ever caught was on the Roanoke River in Virginia. There was a fierce strike and a determined struggle, even as the fish lay in the shallow water at my feet, shaking the offending lure like a fierce dog worrying a bone. And this musky was only three inches long.

I have caught a few larger ones since, but the one that made the biggest impression on me I never caught, never even thought of trying to catch, for when it first caught my eye it was submerged about ten feet down in the clear water of the Delaware, as long as an oar, its eyes fixed, not on our puny lures as they wobbled or

27

spun past its head, but on the stringer of nine or ten bluegills and small bass that hung from the gunwale of our boat. The mental image of a forty-plus pound musky making a surprise hit on that stringer is of the stuff of nightmares, of crocodile attacks and such, but no such thing occurred, as the great fish caught my astonished eye, glared at me analytically, and sank back into its subterranean lair.

The other musky I think of was one I hooked on a small river in Michigan where I have fished, most often with Kevin and various friends of his. He and I were in my canoe, fishing off the edge of a thick weed bed where the bottom shelved off steeply. I had a live minnow and bobber draped over the side, and was taking somewhat disinterested casts into the surrounding open spots in the weeds. It was a sunny afternoon in midsummer, the natural siesta time for much of nature, as well as for human beings who had been up fishing since first light. Then, on the edge of this daydream field of vision, a large fish emerged briefly to investigate my wobbling lure. I finished the retrieve, scarcely believing what I had seen, and quickly cast again. "There's a big old fish in there," I said to Kevin in a semi-whisper, and began another anxious retrieve. This time the fish's appearance was not furtive but furious, with a fierce, rolling strike that whipped the small patch of open water into a foam, which cleared away to reveal my line hopelessly tangled in the thick weeds. We pushed our canoe free of the vegetation and began to clear the weeds away with our paddles while I held the arching rod aloft with my free hand. Finally we worked the fish clear and it exploded on the first of a series of long runs in which I barely kept it free of logs and brush along the shore. For some reason, and with singularly poor judgment, I kept telling Kevin to step out of the canoe and hold it in the current, but the water was just slightly too deep for him to manage it, so we were floating downstream into a narrow, swift place where I felt sure we would lose the fish. I should have just dropped anchor, but I wanted to avoid giving the fish an opportunity to wrap my line around the anchor rope. In any event, I decided we had to try to land it, even though this fish was far from worn out. All we had was a small landing net, and the fish was, in my memory at least, wider than the canoe. I brought it alongside and told Kevin to try to use the net like a shovel to heave it on board. At the critical moment we both heaved, but the fish rolled off the undersized net and hung briefly over the gunwale, long enough for us to see clearly the distinctive vertical musky-bars on its side, and then the great body arched and vaulted clear, leaving the bristling rapala lure silhouetted against the open sky. For a moment we sat transfixed, and then I looked at Kevin to see his face stricken, as I have seen him after striking out in some clutch situation in a baseball game, more so than I have seen when the lost fish was his own, and I knew that, whatever else, this was my friend and fishing brother, to whom my success was indistinguishable from his own, and I thanked the great strong fish for this knowledge, even as I wished intently that we had him on our stringer.

The next Sunday was Father's Day, and Kevin brought me a present: a big long-handled fishing net, which I use to this day.

MUSKELLUNGE

II

Jesus said to his disciples: "no longer do I call you servants . . . but I have called you friends." They were an unlikely bunch, the likes of Mary Magdalene, Simon Peter, Mary and Martha of Bethany, Judas, and John. Many of them were fishermen. Come to think of it, I suspect that one of the reasons Judas got so cross-wise with the rest of them was that he didn't fish. I think he was the deadly serious one, the fiercely earnest and dedicated radical, and probably thought the rest of them were being frivolous to spend so much time out on the lake.

Now Simon Peter, he was the one who under-stood what Jesus was really up to, though like most of us there was a lot more to his insights than he himself realized. He was a rough-hewn man, I'm certain, unschooled in speech and with a penchant for saying the wrong thing at the wrong time. After all, the New Testament says at one point, "and Peter, not knowing what to say, *said* . . ." and you can fill in the blanks, whether it's his proposal to build a nice pilgrimage shrine on the Mount of the Transfiguration, his chopping off ears of the high priests' acolytes, his objections to having his feet washed, or his bitter denial of his friend by the soldiers' campfire. But there was a bond between them, something stronger than Peter's impetuosity or Jesus' transcendent destiny. I can't help but think it had to do with the fishing they did, and still do, in some sense, for in Mark 4:30 Jesus says to Peter (and through him, the church), "deal with people the same way you deal with fishing," or words to that effect. And, after the resurrection, it is on a fishing trip that the Risen Christ manifests himself, prompting Peter to leap one last time into the sea in pursuit of his ubiquitous fishing partner, only to find that Jesus, like the Kwakiutl twin and the salmon, changes forms when he gets too close.

Much has been written, sung, and surmised about Mary Magdalene and her relationship to Jesus. The rock opera *Jesus Christ Superstar* has her singing, "I don't know how to love him," and in so doing speaks for a lot of us, I reckon, who have fallen under his spell and strive together to learn the steps of his sacred dance in our own loud times. I don't know if she ever fished: chances are that even if she didn't she knew a lot about it, since Magdala is a lakeside town. I have to admit that I have not done much fishing with women: some with my daughter Caitlin, some with my wife, some with my sisters. But my sister Kathie now hunts deer with us, and given Caitlin's eagerness, I trust that our fishing circle will soon be made whole and in the male and female image of God, as it should be, as it was among Jesus and his circle, where (in violation of custom and rabbinic statute) women like Mary of Bethany studied Torah at the Rabbi's feet, where the Samaritan woman at the well, the one who caused the disciples to "marvel that Jesus was speaking to a woman" (John 4:23) was taken seriously and sent as an "apostle" to her arche-typically sexist village, and where, in the resurrection garden, to the disreputable woman of Magdala, the Lord and Redeemer of the world appeared to speak her name, simply, as to a friend.

VI

POWER PLACES

"The Lord appeared to Abraham
by the oaks of Mamre"
(Genesis 18:1)

I

Just as certain relationships have a kind of sacramental power, so do certain places. The Book of Genesis is full of allusions to particular spots, hilltops, and groves of trees where sacredness was focused and concentrated. The whole idea of the "Promised Land" partakes of this, and it has its corollaries in my own faith and experience as well.

I speak much of the Delaware River in these stories, and in so doing I am part of a long tradition. The place where we always stayed in the summers is known as Minisink Hills, where Broadheads Creek joins the Delaware just above the Water Gap. The Lenape were the Native American people who lived there, and it was a sacred place to them, as is evidenced by the many burial mounds that have been found. I imagine that they gathered at appointed times to feast and pray there, to dance out their faith, and partake of the bounty of the River and its environs. But they may not have been the first. Once I encountered there a crew from *National Geographic* who were excavating an ancient site which, if their theory proved correct, was the toolyard of a village ten thousand years old, a time that predates most theories of Indian migrations across the Bering Straits. In this long-hallowed place I learned to fish, to grieve for the dead, to fall in love. The summers spent there were the occasions of my most intense adolescent crises and discoveries. And in 1955, in the great flood of that year, our house was swept away and in the night of our escape I saw my father in an expanded light, as a brave leader, trusted by strangers with their lives. That night I knew the River in a new way also, as a remorseless adversary, a monster whispering terror in the dark. It comes, therefore, as no surprise to learn that others have known this as a power place, as holy ground, and have dreamed of it so often that their dreaming merges onto waking life, and the River flows between the worlds, and they are one.

Another sacred place for me exists only in that dreaming world, though it has its outposts on this wakeful side. It is a forest, a deer-haunted woods, where we always go to hunt, but never kill. There is a vague sense of unpreparedness about these dreams: I have forgotten my winter clothing, or my gun, or to get permission to hunt the land. Sometimes there are unexpected transformations, as when the deer elude us by taking refuge in an unlikely luxury hotel, where we are frowned at in our rough hunting clothes and where the deer escape by pretending to be pets. But the overwhelming impression is of a vast, brooding *presence*,

DEER

a hidden potency on whose sufferance alone we are permitted access, and with whom the deer bear some fundamental kinship.

Why do I resort in dreams so often to this place, so eagerly sought after and yet so ominous? I can only guess, though in outward form it resembles the Pennsylvania ridge tops where I have hunted since I was a boy, and where every deer stand assumes in memory or in forethought a measure of its mystery. I can only imagine that in some buried ancestral portion of my mind the deer take on the role of totem animal, of a sacramental creature connecting me to elemental powers obscure to waking thought.

In any event, when the Bible mentions sacred places I think I know whereof it speaks, and I have mixed feelings when the monotheistic party line rails against those who "built them high places and images, and groves, on every high hill, and under every green tree" (1 Kings 14:23 KJV). The Old Testament has a vigorous tension within it between that fierce clarity concerning *Yahweh*, the one true utterly portable God of the desert, and the intensely local divinities called *Baalim* and *Ashtereth*, handy spirits of sacred trees and hilltops, to whose wild festivals the Hebrews felt so strongly drawn, and yet powerfully repelled.

For me this Old Testament dilemma is resolved, as are so many others, within the purview of the New, by Christ, the "icon of the invisible God" as Colossians 1:15 has it, who consecrates sacred space, not in some holy shrine but in the human person.

II

In Eastern Orthodox Christianity, the notion of "icon" is central to both theology and prayer, with the sacred painted images taken to be windows into the eternal, more or less transparent veils cast over the unseen. During the eighth century these Christians refought the ancient battles of the *Baalim* and Hebrew prophets, when the iconoclasts sought to purge the Christian faith of this potential source of superstition, and the iconodules struggled and eventually prevailed with their idea of a God rendered available, however elusively, through the images of the sacred icons.

For my part, I find that the world *swarms* with icons. For me, they are not only pious objects in churches, but can be dreams, rivers, causes and move-ments, and people, yet they are sacramental, indeed windows into a world beyond, and I venerate them as I would a votive-lit shrine in a church. But I also dread these personalized icons, for they have seductive power, and can lull me into a comfortable, self-congratulating piety that is locked in the past and as devoid of spirit as a dusty exhibit in a museum. Over time, they can lose their supple links with the eternal, and become brittle, in fact new idols, opaque against the Living God. When that happens, these familiar icons must be *clasted* (either by me or by some single-minded prophet sent from God), demythologized, or otherwise dispossessed, like the sacred objects of some reformation monastery carried off in the saddlebags of Cromwell's raiders.

Then new icons emerge, are *plasted*, discovered, or discerned, and the cycle of plasting and clasting begins again. Yesterday's sacred icon is tomorrow's idol to be smashed.

Thus I have found that God is always something more than what I had thought, though in truth the process is usually more gentle than what I have implied. As a teenager I was a fiercely partisan Anglo-Catholic, and now that icon has widened out and become more inclusive than I ever would have thought; as a young priest, the social gospel was my burning truth and scourge to use against the ruling powers of this world and the puzzled occupants of church pews, and today I am a more gentle radical, and, I would like to believe, a more effective one. These changes occurred without condescension or denial toward what had gone before, as old icons expanded and then burst, much as a snake sheds skins.

III

Once, after a particularly significant visit with my family in Pennsylvania, I boarded the small plane to begin the trip back to the flat industrial plains of Northwest Indiana. In desolation I viewed the mountain ridges from the plane's window, and found myself thinking of that ancient name for God in Genesis, *El Shaddai*, "Lord of the Mountains," and I grieved for the loss of that mountain sacredness, and the warmth of family. Then it was as if a voice came from a corner of my brain to say: "I AM is my one true name."

And so it is, even in these unpromising lands. For "the One Who Is," *being* is the vehicle of presence: *El Shaddai* is an icon, a family hearth-god stolen by a larger, living name, by *Yahweh*, who through imageless night precedes our fragile flight, just as the fiery pillar receded before the Hebrews at the dawn of faith.

BEAR

VII

RANCID BEARFAT

I

Receded before the Hebrews. All icons behave this way, as does God before the icons.

As I have said, icons can be many things. I usually think of them as weighty and numinous, but not always. Take rancid bearfat, for instance. This obscure substance has been the subject of songs, stories, much speculation, and a small amount of historical research since I learned of it from my Dad, who knew it mainly as a much-sought-after mosquito repellent on fishing trips during his boyhood in east Tennessee. "The bugs hates it wuss than we does," Dad would say, quoting the men who spoke of it around his Daddy's store.

But that's only part of the story. You see, rancid bearfat is so slippery that the mosquitoes slide right off. Furthermore, they pick up so much speed from sliding that it causes them to crash into trees and other obstacles, rendering them unconscious.

Given this property, it is surprising that no

military application has yet been found. I can imagine the possibilities: antiballistic missiles, tipped with warheads containing rancid bearfat, could cause an entire barrage of incoming hostile rockets to go sliding off through outer space at ever-increasing speeds until, approaching the speed of light, they leave the realm of matter behind and there remain forever undetected, as at that velocity the slipperyness of the rancid bearfat increases exponentially, so that even light slides right off. I think it has as much potential as SDI.

The difficulty lies in finding a way to effectively *contain* it. It is so slippery it simply slides right out of whatever container you try to put it in. I've heard it can be frozen at subzero temperatures and stored in cartons very much like ice cream (though God help the person who ever confuses the two). But rancid bearfat can definitely be dangerous to handle: if even the smallest amount gets on the handler, all their clothes slide off. If it gets on their shoes, they begin to slide downhill and, if nothing intervenes, end up in the same state as those ICBMs and mosquitoes. Besides all this, rancid bears are exceedingly difficult to locate in the first place. I was once asked in an interview if rancid bearfat *came* rancid or had to be *synthesized* in some way. I replied that, mercifully, it had to *come* that way as an oversupply could have disastrous results. As it is, rancid bears are extremely difficult to catch or even see, as they slide by so fast they are invisible to all but trained observers.

I was also once asked how there could be any habitat for rancid bears, since any part of the country that came into contact with these creatures would inevitably begin sliding away, leaving nowhere for the rancid bears to be. To this I replied, trying to do justice to my father's methodology, that empiricism was of little value in evaluating this phenomenon, as is evidenced by the ultimate dilemma in rancid bear-lore, the one who somehow gets sliding in a circle until it disappears into itself by a route you might be able to imagine, and having thus rendered itself inaccessible to empirical investigation, poses the perennial philosophical question, Can we speak meaningfully of rancid bears at all? So the elusive trail of the rancid bear leads into the country of the metaphysicians and mystics, where it is best left.

II

Icons, to function, must be slippery. Otherwise they dry up and crumble, though often not before they have done great harm.

Anglicanism has functioned as an icon in my life. It has connected me to God and other people, though with flexible bonds. At the church's knee I learned to live with ambiguity, to value tradition without getting trapped in it, and to reverence the sacred without necessarily feeling threatened by the secular. I also learned social radicalism and the benefit of tolerance, self-criticism and the disciplines of mental health, the value of wisdom and the necessity of humor. It appears that Anglicanism, by accident of politics and history, has stumbled across the awareness that Truth, especially Religious Truth, is slippery, and cannot be successfully boxed, canned, programmed, systematized, or even adequately verbalized, at least for long.

I rejoice in these things, as I urge my parishioners to do, even when they are disgruntled about their church's vagueness as to what it believes in some areas.

Perhaps I shall urge them to conceive of Anglicanism as a slippery icon, sliding reluctantly across history and the earth, eluding anxious idolaters more by sheer velocity than by virtue, leaving a profusion of tea cups, mitres, and revisions of liturgies scattered in its wake.

Upon consideration, however, I will desist in pursuing this analogy further, lest our beloved communion suffer the same fate as the aforementioned metaphysical bear.

> Well rancid bearfat, knows no friction;
> Its long standing legend is stranger than fiction;
> It's greasier than a fish fry, or Elvis's hair;
> It's the rancidist, slipperiest part, of a bear.
> (John Dickson, *Rancid Bearfat*. Used by permission)

VIII

BOATS

Having digressed this far onto the subject of bug repellant, I may as well continue on and tell about boats, which were invented by the same one of our clever ancestors who invented the wheel, I believe. "I-make-box-that-goes-on-water," she probably told her husband, and being the original empiricist, spent a lot of time falling into the water before her invention was a success.

I am impressed by her achievement, as I am by those of her scientific descendants, but to me it is also important to think of a boat (or an automobile, or a train) as not only an expression of human ingenuity, but also an instrument of God's to keep us mindful of our own foolishness.

For instance, I think of an evening about ten years ago when I decided to go fishing. Since it was cool, I had on a nylon winter jacket. I laid my rod and paddle in the canoe and launched it about two-thirds of the way, and proceeded to climb in from the bow. As I did all these things I was thinking of a friend of mine who is very large and has a penchant for falling into various bodies of water. "Ho Ho," I thought, "I am certainly skilled and agile and clever and competent in boats and canoes and stuff." Whereupon the canoe threw me into the pond, as it has done more than once since under similar circumstances.

That reminds me of a watergoing combination of boat and motor we used to have on the Delaware River in days past. The motor was a two-and-a-half horsepower and had to be started by winding a rope around the top and holding the choke in with your thumb while pulling with all your might on the rope. Usually it didn't start, which my father was taking into account one day when he was ferrying a boatload of water-shy aunts and grandmothers across the River to the island where we had our cabin, only to have it start on the first pull and send him head first over the stern with the aunts and the boat chugging confidently downriver toward Philadelphia. The next motor we got, I recall, would also rarely start and was the target of my brother's retaliatory action, which consisted of methodically unfastening it from its moorings on the stern and jettisoning the whole thing in twelve feet of water. And he is a calm person.

But as with all the ambidextrous gifts that God bestows, boats can be vehicles of goodness and grace, as was demonstrated the day I was breaking in a new four horsepower motor on a lake in Wisconsin. I was out with a friend, chugging up and down the shoreline with that little motor when we came upon a drowning drunk. I knew he was drowning because he was screaming at the top of his lungs and sinking below the surface of the lake; I knew he was drunk because I could smell the stale booze in the air even while he was three feet under. We pried him up to the surface with an oar and heaved him into the boat, gave him artificial respiration and wrapped him up with towels, and began trying to decipher his babble about some friends of his who were adrift in a boat somewhere on the lake. After depositing him on the shore, we went to rescue his compatriots, who, as drunk as he had been, solemnly informed us that their friend jumped into the water and sank before their very eyes. We towed them in, and one of them fell out of the boat twice. He gave me two wet dollars and staggered off dripping.

"What a mystery this divine milieu is," I thought. "By some chance I am running an outboard that yesterday I didn't even own on a lake I'd never seen before in just the spot where a man is drowning who is too drunk to know he's been saved."

Talk of boats brings to mind something I've noticed, which is that outboard motors make a kind of musical tone, maybe like the drone of a bagpipe. On the gentle evenings on the Delaware, heading home after fishing, Dad would sit in the stern by that old two-and-a-half horse Firestone with his hand resting easy on the handle and sing in his clear tenor voice, right in key with the motor's drone:

"Summertime, and the livin' is easy,
Fish are jumpin',
And the cotton is high."

And even yet, in the still hours, when I hear the far-off drone of an outboard, I can discern the tune, and the fine, true voice:

"Your Daddy's rich,
and your Mama's good lookin',
So hush little baby,
Don't you cry."*

---

*Song "Summertime" by George Gershwin. c 1935 Chappell & Co. (Renewed). All rights reserved. Used by permission.

IX

PISCATORIAL AND EPISCOPAL REFLECTIONS ON THE SIGNIFICANCE OF LEADERSHIP IN THE CHRISTIAN CHURCH

I am more bossy about fishing than I am almost anything else. Generally speaking, I try to be as collaborative a person as the situation will allow. But when I get out on familiar waters, and am fishing with anyone other than piscatorial peers who are equally experienced there, *I* always take the oars or stern of the canoe, and *I* decide on what water to fish, and give definitive advice on what lures should be used. Positioning the boat is especially important. I want at least somebody to be in a place where they can make the correct presentation to the promising cover at the best angle to the current. *I* want to be the one to determine all that, because one properly presented cast is worth fifty or sixty randomly thrown out every which way. Of course, there is the inevitable situation where a set of complex boat-orientation maneuvers positions an angler for a perfect cast into a tree limb far overhead, which would make the finicky helmsman even more irritated than it does were it not for the fact that the offending cast, as often as not, is his.

My Dad was the same way about boat-positioning, and so is my brother. So was Jesus. Just read John 21:6, where he says: "fish on the *other* side of the boat." Same thing in Luke 5:4. He had a profound understanding of the water, the fish, and the fishermen, and they deferred to him, whether grudgingly or happily we cannot say. In any case, they hauled 'em in.

I have learned or am in the process of learning, that being bossy rarely pays off, either on the water or elsewhere. I have often been humbled and instructed by those who, as Psalm 119 says, are "wiser than [their] elders." My young fishing partner Kevin has a friend

who used to be small for his age but, like Jesus, had a real sense for the fish. On one occasion we were fishing and he tied on a really bizarre-looking chartreuse spinner bait of a variety I have always disparaged. I could see the thing glowing in the water the entire length of his cast. "Take the net out on the bank and wait for the fish there," I told him magisterially, "because that thing is going to scare them all out of the creek." No sooner had I spoken than a very visible bass struck the very visible lure, a phenomenon I have observed since while using similar lures myself, though I still can't bring myself to use the fluorescent colors. That same boy unwittingly prophesied against my pretensions one day when we were fishing upstream on a hot afternoon and, the current being brisk, I got tired of paddling and set Kevin's diminutive friend to towing us manually in the knee-deep water. Knee-deep on *me*, that is, and getting gradually deeper, a fact that Kevin and I overlooked as we were casting into some inviting cover along the shore. When I did glance forward I saw the bow line angling downward into the water, and I could feel the canoe still surging upstream, but all I could see of the boy was his hat! Every so often he would surface and blow for air like a whale. I hastened to call him out of the water, but the incident stuck in my mind as an example of obedience carried to unadvisable extremes. So I have made efforts to move toward shared decision making, though I am still loathe to give up the stern position in the canoe.

Jesus was not an authoritarian leader. His strong, assertive manner was the means of creating freedom in others, not of fostering a kind of immobilizing dependence upon him.* Which is a good thing, since after the Resurrection he absented himself from the scene to assume a universal and exalted role, leaving the church to continue as "fishers of men," though not, of course, unassisted.

This has been a roundabout way of slipping up on the subject of *bishops*, partly because it seemed to fit in sequence with bugs, bears, and boats, but mostly because bishops are very important to Episcopalians and to me, and these reflections may have helped illuminate the whole subject of leadership in a Christian context. In Anglicanism generally, bishops have more symbolic authority than they do administrative power. The most authentic leaders amongst the bishops I have dealt with in my ministry have been people who, like Jesus, exhibit both strength and vulnerability, and struggle against the isolation from reality that results from people's tendency to award them either cheap grace or cheap shots. The office they bear and incarnate is that of Apostle, of witness to the Resurrection, passed on tangibly and tactually by the laying on of hands, like some great historical line-dance, or like the Plains Indians to whom

*To be theologically accurate, there is a sense in which we are *utterly* dependent upon Christ, but even that dependence is used by God to create freedom in us.

"the Medicine Wheel way begins with the touching of our brothers and sisters" (Storm 1978). To be ordained in this sequence is to be caught up in the dance, "touched in the head," as it were, like David who danced like a fool before the Ark of God. This is the Apostolic Succession, and it is *myth*, in the terms I have been using in these stories. The reality is often more mundane, but their intersection, like the meeting of a bass with a chartreuse spinner bait, is an occasion of grace and power.

For me, an example of this intersection comes from the body of stories I tell about my friend C. I. Jones, who is now a bishop but whom I came to know over many hours spent following his exemplary old bird dog around fields and woods in search of quail or grouse. But we have never fished.

Ci does not like to fish, as I learned in the early days of our acquaintance when we were participating in one of those spiritual retreats where there is a rigorous silence observed and people stand around before meals in oversized monastic-type rooms and prepare to eat in self-conscious silence while being read to out of some edifying book. In this particular case, Ci and I were whispering to each other in front of a large fireplace about guns and birds and deer, keeping our voices very low so as not to disturb the devout thoughts of our colleagues. "I don't like to fish," Ci whispered in his North Carolina mountain drawl. "I can't see thrashing around after an ugly critter like that." "But Ci," I whispered back, "a fish is a beautiful creature to behold." "AN OLD SLIMY FEESH!" Ci burst out, an utterance which set us at once to gazing intently at the fire in hasty repentance for having distracted the meditations of our brothers and sisters.

Now that Ci is a bishop, I conceive of all such folk as carrying somewhere on their person an old slimy feesh. This could be said as well of bishops, teachers, parents, or other bearers of mythic power. That feesh is their reality, their vulnerable humanity, their uncensored self that blurts out truth at unguarded moments, and they can deal with it in several ways: they can try to ignore it; they can lie about it; they can pretend it's some kind of vestment; or they can accept it, even show it off a little, provided that it's always done "decently and in order," of course.

Thus the myth and the reality may intersect, the "touching of our brothers and sisters" be accomplished, and we can "look upon and touch with our hands . . . that which was from the beginning" (1 John 1:1).

X

EUCHARIST

It amazes me that there are people who keep fish but don't eat them. I can't say that all forms of aquatic life are equally appetizing, but I cannot imagine keeping a fish that I did not at least intend to consume. It's like going to Mass and declining to receive communion. It's a kind of sacred obligation I owe to the fish for offering itself, and to the whole creation process of which we are privileged to partake. In most cases, it's no great sacrifice, such as when Mark Johnston fries up spanish mackerel from the Gulf with hush puppies on the side, or when I poach fresh-caught pike fillets in foil with lemon and butter on the coals of a campfire.

There are times when the principle is stretched, however, as once when I was camping with some friends and we had not brought much food with us at all. I had hoped to catch fish for us to eat, but they proved uncooperative until I hooked a large dogfish back in a goose-haunted bayou. The fish was big enough to tow our canoe, and I remarked, "Well boys, we are going to find out what dogfish tastes like tonight," but this was

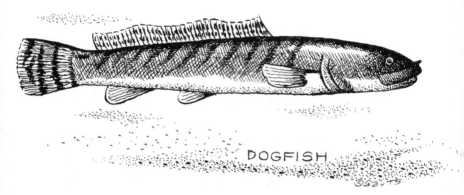

DOGFISH

not to be, because the fish gave a strong surge and straightened out the hook, thus absolving us of the experience of eating dogfish.

Jesus ate fish all the time, and is the only leader of a great religious movement to have made a sacrament out of a fish fry. That may seem far-fetched, but all four gospels attest to the fact that Jesus fed large groups of people with minuscule amounts of food, the food being Palestinian panfish and the inevitable bread.

To the early church this event was closely identified with the Eucharist, wherein the many partake of the inexhaustible resources of the One.

Our own Eucharistic life is modeled on this as well. The feeding episodes reveal God's economic order: *you put in what you can and get back what you need*. We come to the Eucharist each Sunday much like those who came out to hear Jesus in the lonely places, ill-provisioned and preoccupied with private needs, and there are fed in ways beyond our knowing, and thus leave our crowd identity behind and become partakers of a Commonwealth which is in heaven. From the table we are sent out empowered to extend this divine prodigality into the world.

Sometimes at communion time the supply of consecrated bread runs low, and I begin to doubt that there is enough to go around, and still the people press forward, stretching out their hands. In my parish, there is a fondness for old evangelical hymns, and the people will sometimes sing from memory as they kneel at the altar rail, songs such as, "I Need Thee Every Hour" and "Just As I Am," and to my eyes the walls of the church seem to expand and the rail extends out over the horizon and fills with people, living and dead, known and unknown, all singing and reaching out their hands in their thousands toward the mercy and generosity of God and I look at the pitiful supply of hosts and wonder, "what are they among so many?"

But there is one to feed them, and the hymn ends, the walls of the church contract, and the people emerge to the inevitable doughnuts and coffee, their eyes squinting against the brighter light, like bewildered apostles from an empty tomb.

FIRST COMMUNION

I

In April, starting from some hidden ocean place,
The Shad column
Makes its long-remembered way
Up riffles and the steeply slanting rocks
That form the Delaware
To where
We fish
Aiming casts like missiles from some foreign land,
Plotted to intersect
Trajectories unseen.

By our crafted violence thus
We bait the iridescent pinkish silver power,
The flat-sided strength
Turned counter-current
In the High Spring's flood.

II

And by another craft and deep place
Boundered by old stone and blue glass
We cast out our hands,
In hopes to intersect again
the streaming fish-host,
To feed on flashing pink and silver,
the Atlantic, the Unseen,
And having fed, find power so as to fish again
On the wide flowing River of the World.

JCS+ June 2 1987

XI

FIRST COMMUNIONS

I wrote that poem on the occasion of my nephew Ben's first communion, which, for one reason or another, had taken place somewhat later than is the usual practice in the Episcopal Church today. He and his Dad had gone on a shad-fishing expedition to the Delaware River the weekend before, and to me there was an affinity between the two events. Hence the poem.

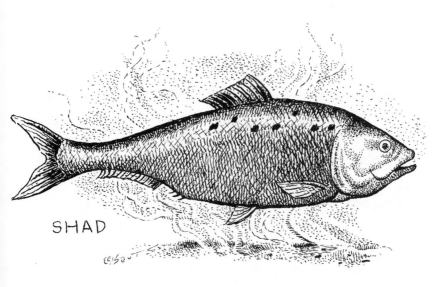

SHAD

More comes to mind for me. I think of all my initiations, my comings-of-age, my passages. I think of drivers licenses, of ordinations, and of the deep communion of trust and intimate discovery that I have shared with Cheri, my wife. And I think of deer hunting in Pennsylvania, and my Grandfather, and the Camp where I went every deer season during my high school years, and where I underwent both great humiliation and, I now believe, great learning.

I was the child of a liberal upbringing, a city boy unschooled in the more traditional etiquette of youth and age that prevailed among my mother's Pennsylvania kin. I am also a painfully slow learner, though I didn't think so then. The men at Deer Camp were gruff, plainspoken, and competent. They explained things once and expected them to be done from henceforth in their way. I do not listen well to directions, and found ways to make every mistake that could possibly be made. When I drew water I did it too hastily and riled the spring; I cussed inappropriately, not having earned the right to that mode of eloquence; I dropped my rifle barrel-first in the mud; and most of all, I was always misunderstanding instructions and getting in the wrong place in the woods, creating a potentially dangerous situation and messing up our drives.

I should add that while I was stumbling through my initiation in the woods, I was also picking up a great deal of deer-lore. These men really knew the deer, and the woods, and respected both. I think some of this unspoken reverence rubbed off on me, even as I was preoccupied trying to endure the daily dose of criticism which, I believed, I richly deserved.

Except for one thing that happened: we were on one of our regular deer drives where the standers string out along a creek bed and the drivers make a long sweep across a scrub oak barren toward them. The drivers at our camp always moved very quietly through the woods, not shouting or barking or blowing whistles, as I have seen others do since. At our camp, we were not even permitted to speak above a whisper while in the woods, which gave the whole enterprise a kind of liturgical flavor. In any event, I was one of the drivers, and as usual, got lost, though I didn't know it. I was to drive straight across the barren till I came to a drop off, then cut right along the base of it till I saw a stander. That seemed simple enough, but the terrain was irregular and I ended up walking parallel to the line of standers. Without being aware of making any steep descent, I found myself at the foot of an incline in some open hardwoods, where I saw one of my grown cousins advancing toward me. I took him for one of the standers, but in fact he was the driver on the far end of our drive, and I had been about the wander clear off our hunting area. "Where the hell you think you're going," he whispered harshly. "I'm supposed to follow the base of that ridge," I offered lamely. "This isn't where you're supposed to be," he said. "Just follow me down this way." He turned to continue on through the woods but paused and turned back to say in a louder voice: "and you're no hunter, that's for sure."

I'm glad to say that in subsequent seasons at Deer Camp things improved for me. I learned to adapt to the mores of Camp life, got lost much less, and killed a good buck on a stand of my own choosing. The last year I went, my junior year in high school, I also missed a very large buck when the firing pin of my rifle was broken and I watched harmlessly as the deer passed within twenty-five yards of me and I shucked unfired cartridges onto the forest floor. The thing is that I felt no regret, no sense of failure, but only a curious sense of connection to the animal. It was the last year that Granddad was able to go to Camp, and I never returned.

Years later, my brother and I decided we would try some deer hunting on our own in a different part of the state. He had little experience at it, and the only methods I knew were drawn from my years at Deer Camp, where we always had a large group and hunted the same terrain every year in ritualized, traditional patterns of driving and standing. So Bob and I had to improvise.

This hunting was different in more ways than one. Bob and I ascribe to a different theory of learning, you might say. We believe that people learn best in a climate of trust and support, where it's OK to try new things and make mistakes, and emotional honesty is more important than saving face and gentle self-deprecation replaces ridicule. We also look out for each other in the woods, and know each other's mental habits so well that with only a few words we can gain a clear picture of the other's intentions. And so we set out to devise our own method of deer hunting. After several days of hunting unproductive-looking mountainsides we came across a wide area of scrub and stubby trees, a burned over place most likely, and concentrated our hunting there. It was the second week of the Season, so there were few other hunters in the woods. On our last day to hunt, a light snow had fallen, and the weather was warming. Speaking in whispers, as I had been taught to do, we planned a simple, two-man drive. While he stood beneath a huge old pine, I made my circuit through the barren, moving stealthily, thinking of my rough old cousins and their ways. About half way through my drive I came to a sort of run way through the brush, and, in the fresh snow, three sets of new deer tracks, headed straight for the tall pine where my brother stood watching. Unexpectedly, I thought of those harsh words spoken to me twenty years before: "You're no hunter," words I had not remembered for a long, long time. And then, looking at the tracks, I thought of Bob and saw through his eyes the passing gray shapes, the almost miraculous-seeming appearance of deer among the myriad familiar forms of rocks and trees and sky. "Oh, yes I am too," I thought. "Not as skilled, not as experienced, not the same way that those men were hunters, but a hunter all the same, in *my* way, in *our* way."

Since then we have killed a number of deer, while many others slipped away. In recent years young hunters are joining us, and we try to teach them. We undoubtedly make our own mistakes and commit our own brand of sins against them which they will someday have to overcome in some new context of their own. In this manner they will seek their own communion, on the wide flowing river of the world.

XII

" . . . Into an Open Place"
(Psalm 18:20)

Winfield Scott was thirteen when he died, drowned in Broadheads Creek where it joins the Delaware. I was part of the search party that combed the surrounding woods in hopes of finding him alive, a lost camper from a summer camp long since closed. Then the divers came, and they found him washed beneath the remains of an old railroad bridge. They laid him on the dock at my feet. I was sixteen that summer, and it was my first experience with death.

Years later I returned to Pennsylvania to take part in my Grandmother's funeral, and spent the early part of the day fishing the same spot where Winfield had been found. It is a familiar spot to me, and I had fished it many times before. The River flows swiftly there, and I stood knee deep in chest waders, fishing downstream toward the deep holes around the old railroad bridge. As I turned upstream to seek a new casting point I lost my footing on the slick rocks. In an instant the waders filled with cold water, stealing my breath. I felt the power of the River sliding me down toward the deep hole. In my head I was calculating the comparative risks in trying to peel the waders off so I could swim, or else trying to reach shallow water with the waterlogged waders still on. It didn't matter, it turned out, because I suddenly found myself beached on the dry rocks, propelled thither, I suppose, by own churning feet, which had not waited for my head to form its well-laid plan.

Since then I have been more cautious about using chest waders, of course, but I have thought of this incident for other reasons too. I have thought of Winfield, whom I never knew in life, and of my Grandmother, and of the River which very nearly joined us all that day, there where the Creek and River meet.

And once, in a kind of meditative dream, I supposed that I had drowned there on that day, and felt myself merging with the flow, until my fingers touched the sources of high creeks far above, and my feet were washed by Atlantic tides. Then I was a trout, a huge old Brown, holding myself suspended in the current with only the slightest motion of my fins. Then, in my fish-incarnation I beheld the shore, and saw a Man and Boy making preparations to go fishing. I knew their identities: the man was my brother Bob; the other his son Ben, at that time yet unborn.

Years later still, as my father lay dying, I read out loud from the appointed Psalm:

The breakers of death rolled over me,
and the torrents of oblivion made me afraid.
I called upon the Lord in my distress
and cried out to my God for help.
He mounted on cherubim and flew;
he swooped on the wings of the wind.
He wrapped darkness about him;
he made dark waters and thick clouds his pavilion.
The beds of the seas were uncovered,
and the foundations of the earth laid bare . . .

Dad, who was much weakened in the advanced stages of cancer, raised himself up and cried in a loud voice, "The Boatman!" And a few moments later he was gone.

He reached down from on high and grasped me;
he drew me out of great waters.
He brought me out into an open place . . .
(Psalm 18: 11, 12, 16-17, 20a, *Book of Common Prayer*)

Since then I have witnessed (and, I hope, assisted) the birth of our two children, and been amazed at the great gush of water that carries them headlong into this waiting world; they literally ride the rapids into the future. They are no strangers to water, nor is their mother. Now I feel I know the source of my recurrent dreams of deep, clear lakes which, for some reason, always evoke a sense of my mother's presence, and of the profound reverence (along with jolly companionship and downright raucous joy) which I feel for Cheri, my wife, for she is a River.

And in my priestly role I have baptized many people, old and young, in lakes and more often fonts, have stood myself (or rather been held in the arms of others), one of a long line of pilgrims, with Jesus at the head, while they wade into that River of wisdom, and a choir chants in Hebrew, and a dove circles overhead.

In the end, the River comes into an open place, which I recognize. Dad is there, teaching Winfield Scott how to fish; Gramma is on the shore, stoking up a fire to cook their catch. Jesus is bringing her firewood. There is a rumor of rancid bears in the woods. Karoks dance along the shore.

I know the place. It is Chickenbone Lake, where the fish are always hungry, the water always clear, and the pines keep watch along the shore.

LIST OF WORKS CITED

Burland, Cottie. Revised by Marion Wood. *North American Indian Mythology*. New York: Peter Bedrick Books, 1985.

Frazer, Sir James. *The Golden Bough*. Vol. 1. Abr. Ed. New York: Macmillan, 1963.

Stevenson, R. Taylor. "History as Myth: Some Implications for History and Theology." *Cross Currents* (1970).

Storm, Hyemeyohosts. *Seven Arrows*. New York: Ballentine Books, 1978.

ORDER BLANK

Please send me _____ copies of *Chickenbone Lake: Myths, Fishing Stories, and Theological Asides*, @ $6.00 each.

Please add $1.25 shipping charges for the first item, and $.35 for each additional item.

Indiana residents add 5% sales tax.

Make checks payable to:

Anadromous Press
Box 604
Griffith, IN   46319

Your name: _____

Address: _____

City _____ State _____ Zip _____